Traveling With The Angels

Journey To Find The Real Me

H. Sanaé

Balboa Press books may be ordered through booksellers or by contacting:

Balboa Press
A Division of Hay House
1663 Liberty Drive
Bloomington, IN 47403
www.balboapress.com
1 (877) 407-4847

Interior Graphics/Art Credit
Dr. Sunnaquair D Chen
Tom Kimura.P

ISBN: 978-1-9822-0762-5 (sc)
ISBN: 978-1-9822-0761-8 (e)

Library of Congress Control Number: 2018907735

Print information available on the last page.

Balboa Press rev. date: 07/12/2018

BALBOA.
PRESS
A DIVISION OF HAY HOUSE

1. NOWHERE

2. CALLING

3. IF ONLY I COULD

4. WHEN I WAS FIVE

5. RIGHT HERE

1. NOWHERE
(#001 - #012)

Let me put my earphones on.
So I can shut out the rest of the world.

There's no one to turn to.
I got nothing to do, but cry.

But music never lets me down.

I don't feel anything, but my body screaming.
Crashing. Crashing. Tell me why I'm still here?

Because I belong nowhere I give into loneliness.

Music only heals my pain.
The medicine ain't working. (Ain't working.)

Let me put my earphones on.
So I can shut out the rest of the world.

There's no job I want to do.
I got nothing to do, but sleep.

But music never lets me down.

I knew this was coming, but my ego denying.
Dying. Dying. Tell me why I'm still here?

Because I belong nowhere I give into loneliness.

Music only heals my pain.
The medicine ain't working. (Ain't working.)

2. CALLING
(#013 - #020)

How long have I been hiding in this shell?
I hear you calling, "come out baby." (Come out baby.)

Crying all day all night. Staring at the ceiling.
Questioning myself everyday like "is it worth my tears?"

A whispering voice from up above.
"Take the first step so everything will change."

"The miracles are yet to come."

How long have I been pretending like I'm somebody else?
I see your helping hand, "it's safe here." (It's safe here.)

Thinking all day all night. Looking at the window.
Questioning myself everyday like "is it worth my tears?"

An unknown letter from up above.
"Come join us so everything will change."

"The miracles are yet to come."

3. IF ONLY I COULD

(#021 - #031)

"Congratulations" with a fake smile.
How can I be happy for someone's success?

Everyone looking so happy here, but me.

Feeling miserable like a failure. How did it all begin?

Signs are everywhere. (I know)
My heart knows what it wants. (You know)

If only I could get a chance, I would come up on that stage singing.

"You did a great job" with a beautiful lie.
What else am I supposed to say?

Everyone looking so happy here, but me.

Never felt like I fit in anywhere. Where did it all begin?

Signs are everywhere. (I know)
My heart knows what it wants. (You know)

If only I could get a chance, I would come up on that stage singing.

So what is stopping me?

4. WHEN I WAS FIVE
(#032 - #041)

-You left me in the dark when I was five.

That night I should have trusted my feeling.

A sudden call. Stomach dropped.
A midnight long plane ride. (*Flashback. Flashback.*)

That night I should have stayed at home.

Cold hands. Brain shocked.
A little white cloth on his face. *(Flashback. Flashback.)*

I've hidden my pain so well until I met you.
Why is a tear dropping from my eye?

How could it be possible? You were just a stranger.
That I met on the airplane. *(Seat 37. Seat 37.)*

But you reminded me of that person...

Who left me in the dark when I was five.

Is it weird if I call you grandpa?
So I can say my last goodbye to him.

5. RIGHT HERE

(#042 - 050)

Feet in the sand looking at the ocean.
It wasn't easy, but I've made it this far.

People have come and gone *(He tried. She tried)*
They asked me what to do *(I tried. I tried.)*

I became the person I was expected to be.
But the more I played it safe, the harder my life became.

Because at the end of the day.
That was not the real me. *(The real me)*

You know what? I didn't change.
I just got lost to be found.

But I needed the key to my heart.
Before I started a new life.

Now I'll sing this song for you.
So let's stop right here. **(Right here.)**

Because nobody, but you. *(But you.)*
Have the key to your heart, but you.

Light through the trees. A sign from above.
Are you ready for a new life?

Acknowledgement

Firstly, I would like to acknowledge and thank everyone who was involved in this project and have supported me throughout the process as well as Balboa Press that helped me to push forward.

There are many people I would like to show my gratitude to especially;

My little sister who is an aspiring singer songwriter, Nachi for collaborating with me to use a part of my book at a live music show, which gave me the courage to share my story in public.

Tom for assisting me during some of my darkest times through the process, giving me inspiration for the design, and being a huge support in my musical journey.

My beautiful friends from college, Geneva, Samantha, and Yaly for keeping me motivated and helping me with my English, editing and proofreading since day 1 of college.

Julian for giving me professional advice on my book or any projects I was working on to be successful as well as my entire career since I started my translation work.

Denise whom I call a twin soul sister that I met in my angel intuitive class for being my total inspiration and sharing signs from the angels with me, that gave me reassurance.

My best friend from elementary school, Sara for supporting me and my project in any way she could such as traveling together and lending me a space to work on my book.

My parents, Hiroyuki and Ayako and my little brother, Takuro for being a big support system especially after the car accident and trusting me to handle all of the hard work.

My previous coworkers for making me realize the pattern I was creating that stopped me from doing what I love by showing me their dedicated work ethic and passion.

Doreen Virtue for all of her spiritual guidance and teaching us the angel intuitive course in Maui, which encouraged me to take the first step that became a life changing experience.

Dennis for helping me with my photos by traveling around the Big Island together, and making my trip very special that also helped me to heal my past pain to move forward.

Finally, I would like to say a special thank you to all of my behind the scenes help and inspiration:

Aria Narang (singer/songwriter), Michelle McClellan, Michael Floyd Shanks (musician), Kana and Thomas (The Aeolian Residence), Liki Braz (V&S O'Polynesia Gifts - weaver/artist) Lea (Dennis's granddaughter), and Dr. Dennis Chen (photographer). Dr. Chen, known as Sunnaquair, was sent into my life by the angels to inspire many of my songs. He is also the artist behind many of the photos within this book. Please visit his website in support! http://flickr.com/photos/sunnaquair/

About the author

Sanaé, born and raised in Japan, is passionate about writing, "oracle cards.", traveling, photography, and music. Her car accident in 2016 awakened psychic abilities she rejected since her teenage years, and she's now a certified Angel Intuitive. With her 4 years of studying abroad in the U.S., she works as a Japanese-English translator/Interpreter, and she is also composing songs like that within this book to fulfill her heart's true desire. "For information on Sanaé's work, please visit her at www.travelingwiththeangels.com/"

A list of the places of the photos
(All taken in the Big Island, HI) :

#001 #004 #050 : Historic Mango Grove, Kapoho
#002 #005 #014 #018 #023 #028 #036 #045 : Pu'uhonua o Hōnaunau National Historical Park, Hōnaunau
#003 #006 #008 #010 #030 #037 #038 #039 #043 #044 #048 : Kona Bay
#007 #009 #012 #016 #025 : Ahalanui Hot Pond
#011 : Daniel K. Inouye Memorial Highway
#013 : Hulihe'e Palace, Kona
#015 #017 #019 #020 #021 #022 #024 #029 #040 : Michelle's place, Kapoho
#026 #027 : V & S O'Polynesia Gifts, Kona
#031 #042 #046 : Kehaha Kai State Park, Kona
#032 Dennis's granddaughter, Lea
#033 Captain Cook
#034 Kona International Airport
#035 #049 The Aeolian Residence, Waikoloa Village
#041 #047 Dennis's Place, Kona

All photos except for #013, #022, #032, #033, #034, #035, #038, #039, #041, #049 were taken by Dr. Sunnaquair D Chen. The photos with the number provided were taken by the author, Sanaé

Printed in the United States
By Bookmasters